Bite At Twilight Cookbook
Vampires, Forks, and Knives

Also by author Gina Meyers, *The Magic of Bewitched Cookbook, The Magic of Bewitched Trivia and More, The Magic of Bewitched Trivia book, and Love At First Bite, The Unofficial Twilight Cookbook.*

Bite At Twilight Cookbook
Vampires, Forks, and Knives

Gina Meyers

Serendipity Media
California

Bite At Twilight Cookbook
Vampires, Forks, and Knives

Copyright © 2009 by Gina Meyers
All rights reserved. No part of this book may be used or reproduced by any means, graphic, electronic, or mechanical,
including photocopying, recording, taping or by any information storage retrieval system without the written permission of the publisher except in the case of brief quotations embodied in critical articles and reviews.

Serendipity Press books may be ordered online or by contacting:
Serendipity Media Group
P.O. Box 26734
Fresno, Ca. 93729
http://serendipitypressinc.blogspot.com/
serendipitypressinc@gmail.com

Because of the dynamic nature of the Internet, any Web addresses or links contained in this book may have changed since publication and may no longer be valid. The views expressed in this work are solely those of the author and do not necessarily refect the views of the publisher, and the publisher hereby disclaims any responsibility for them.
ISBN: 978-0-615-28295-4 (pbk)
Printed in the United States of America
Serendipity Media rev. date: 5/8/09

Book front and back cover concept and design by, David Lawrence Meyers. Hand model for front cover, Lauren Rose Meyers. All rights reserved.

Bite At Twilight Cookbook
Vampires, Forks, and Knives
Table of Contents

Easy Twilight Trivia……………………………………........ 2
The Twilight Movie Cast……………………………..………………....... 4
Bite at Dawn (Breakfast)………………………………..…. 5
There are Cold-Cut Sandwiches in the fridge (light fare, sandwiches, and salads)……………………………………………........6
Get Out the Forks and Knives (Main Meals)…………………13
Chow Bella (Flavorful Italian dishes)……………………....24
Bite at Twilight (Desserts)…Best served cold…………….31
Love at First Sip (non-alcoholic Beverages)……………….49
Howl at Twilight (Cocktails)……………………………….55
Cutting down on the fat……………………………………69
Ways to lighten up a recipe………………………………...70
Substitutions……………………………………………..…70
Weights and measures……………………………………...71
Cooking terms and translations …………………………….73
Index…………………………………………………….….74
Twilight Party Planning Guide……………………………..78
Bella's Prom Primer Checklist……………………………...81
About the author…………………………………….…..….85

Introduction

The international phenomenon known as Twilight fever has ignited excitement in the kitchen. Delectable delights to satisfy the appetites of the humans found in the fictional book *Bite At Twilight: Vampires, Forks, & Knives*, is meant to offer a satisfying array of warm, lovely dishes that anyone of any age can cook with ease and enjoyment.

Whether you are planning a Twilight-Themed Birthday Party, just a simple get together with friends, a Halloween party, or just what to try your creative hand to some culinary delights you are in luck. Filled with forbidden love, action, and danger, brace yourself, and bring your very best table manners, and appetites. Don't forget your forks. Beautiful Bella Swan will be serving up some scrumptious delights to satisfy even the pickiest, puritan "vegetarian" vampires. Intertwined in the pages of *Bite At Twilight Cookbook: Vampires, Forks, & Knives*, you will find Bell's Lasagna, Harry's Famous Fish Fry, Mushroom Raviolis, Red Velvet Cake, Blushing Bella Punch, and much more. Besides mouthwatering recipes, you'll also find a Twilight Party Planning Guide, and for the teenagers, Bell's Prom Primer.

Easy Twilight Trivia

1. What is Bella's first name?
   A. Isabella
   B. Bellina
   C. Alexandra

2. Name Bella's dad?
   A. Henry
   B. Phil
   C. Charlie

3. What is their last name?
   A. Duck
   B. Swan
   C. Goose

4. What does Bella's dad do for a living?
   A. He is a commercial fisherman
   B. He is a fireman
   C. He is a police chief

5. Name the town Bella's dad resides?
   A. Seattle, Washington
   B. Forks, Washington
   C. Spoons, Nevada

6. Bella's car is a red
   A. Old Chevy truck
   B. BMW
   C. Toyota Tundra

7. Bella recently left what town to be closer to her dad?
   A. Phoenix, Arizona

B. Dallas, Texas
C. Tuscon, Arizona

8. Bella's dad lives in a:
   A. Small town
   B. Big city
   C. The suburbs

9. Edward is a cute guy, who happens to be?
   A. A werewolf
   B. A vampire
   C. A warlock

10. The Cullen clan, calls themselves?
    A. Vegetarians
    B. Carnivores
    C. Typical Vampires, "I want to suck your blood."

Answers: 1) A; 2. C; 3) B; 4) C; 5) B; 6) A; 7) A; 8) A; 9) B; 10) A

The Twilight Movie Cast

Kristen Stewart	Bella Swan
Robert Pattison	Edward Cullen
Billy Burke	Charlie Swan
Ashley Green	Alice Cullen
Nikki Reed	Rosalie Hale
Jackson Rathbone	Jasper Hale
Kellan Lutz	Emmett Cullen
Peter Facinelli	Dr. Carlisle Cullen
Cam Gigandet	James
Taylor Lautner	Jacob Black
Anna Kendrick	Jessica Stanley
Michael Welch	Mike Newton
Christian Serratos	Angela Weber
Gil Birmingham	Billy Black
Elizabeth Reaser	Esme Cullen

"It would be more…prudent for you not to be my friend. But, I'm tired of trying to stay away from you Bella." -Edward

Bite at Dawn (Breakfast)

"Breakfast time, he said casually kidding and you said I couldn't act."- Edward talking to Bella

"Breakfast for the human, milk and cereal".-Edward

Charlie's fried eggs
2 eggs
1 Tablespoon of Butter or margarine
Salt and pepper to taste
EASY

Directions: In a skillet, melt butter or margarine over medium heat. Once the butter has melted, crack two eggs into the skillet and cook. With a spatula, once the egg whites have started to turn a golden color, flip. Salt and pepper to taste.

"Last night I'd discovered Charlie couldn't cook much besides fried eggs and bacon."-Bella

Eggs Benedict
3 English muffins
6 slices broiled ham
6 poached eggs
Hollandaise Sauce
EASY

Directions: Split and toast English muffins. Cut ham and place on the English muffin, slip egg on top of ham and smother with hollandaise sauce. Serve hot. Makes 6.

Eggs Bellentine
1 package, 10 ounces of chopped frozen spinach
¼ cup of butter or margarine
2 Tablespoons of flour
2 cups of half and half
8 eggs poached
Shredded Cheddar cheese and grated Parmesan cheese
Salt and pepper to taste
MEDIUM

Directions: Poach eggs and cook frozen spinach according to the package instructions. To prepare the white sauce, melt the butter or margarine in a saucepan, add flour, stir in the half and half. Stir the mixture often, making sure it becomes bubbly. Next, place the spinach in a lightly buttered shallow baking dish. Arrange eggs over the top of the spinach, then pour white sauce over eggs. Sprinkle cheese over the mixture, and, if desired, salt and pepper. Bake in a 400 degree oven for 3 minutes, until cheese is melted.

There are Cold-Cut Sandwiches (in the fridge)

Corned Beef Sandwich
2 slices bread
Softened butter
2 slices cooked corned beef
Prepared mustard

Directions: Spread bread with butter. Place corned beef in the middle of the two bread slices and add spread mustard on the corned beef.

Club Sandwich
2 slices bread
Butter
2 slices cold chicken
Mayonnaise
2 crisp slices of bacon
2 slices of tomato
EASY

Directions: Toast bread and spread with butter on one slice and mayonnaise on the other piece of bread. Add chicken, tomato, and bacon to the center of the sandwich.

Bella prepares grilled cheese sandwiches for her dad Charlie, Billy Black and Jacob, Billy's son.

Jacob Blacks Grilled Cheese Sandwich
White or cheddar cheese, thinly sliced
Margarine or Butter
White or wheat Bread

Skillet
EASY

Directions: Spread margarine or butter on either side of a white or wheat piece of bread. Place cheese in the middle of the bread, close the sandwich. In a skillet on low heat, lightly brown both sides of the bread till the cheese is melted.

Ham and Apple Sandwich
½ cup apple butter
2teaspoon onion
½ teaspoon mustard
Raisin bread, toasted
A slice of ham
Cheese (provolone , Swiss, or Monterey jack)
Red apples, sliced
MEDIUM

Directions: Toast the raisin bread. Thinly slice the apples, cheese. When the toast is cool, adds mustard and chopped onions to one side of the toast. On the other slice, place the apple butter and apple slices. Lastly, add the ham and cheese to the sandwich.

"..So I requested to be assigned kitchen detail."-Bella describing her dad's lack of cooking skills

Tuna Sandwich

2 slices of Sourdough bread, toasted
1 can of water based tuna, drained
¼ cup of mayonnaise
1 sweet pickle, diced
1 celery stalk, finely chopped
MEDIUM

Directions: Mix ingredients in a bowl and place in between the two pieces of toasted bread. There will be leftover tuna mix, enough to make two more sandwiches.

"What if I'm not the hero? What if I'm the bad guy?"-Edward

Monster Eggs

6 hard boiled eggs
¼ cup of mayonnaise
1 teaspoon of mustard
1 teaspoon of red wine vinegar
Paprika to dash
MEDIUM

Directions: Hard boil eggs. When cooled, remove shell and cut lengthwise and remove yolks. Place yolks in a bowl and mash, add the mayonnaise, mustard, and vinegar. Once mashed, place yolk mixture in egg white and dash with paprika.

"Will you turn into a bat?"-Bella

"Like I've never heard that one before."-Edward

Bat Chips
1 large flour tortilla
Cooking spray
Bat Cookie cutouts
Salt (optional)
MEDIUM

Directions: Preheat broiler to low. Using a bat shaped cookie cutter, press out bat shapes on the tortilla. Spray cookie sheet with cooking spray and broil tortillas until they turn crispy and brown colored. May sprinkle with salt. Depending on the size of the bat cookie cutter, one large flour tortilla yields approximately four bat chips.

Salad a la Cullen
Butter lettuce
Sliced strawberries
Sliced grapes
Sliced apples
4 ounces of vanilla or lemon yogurt
Honey roasted peanuts
1 Tablespoon honey
2 Tablespoon vinegar
1 Tablespoon olive oil
Salt and pepper to taste
MEDIUM

Directions: Mix the ingredients together. Place lettuce on a plate and decorate with the fruit and sprinkle with honey roasted nuts.

Broccoli Raisin Salad
1 purple onion, thinly sliced
1 package of fresh broccoli florets
1 cup golden raisins
1 cup mayonnaise
4 bacon slices, cooked and crumbled
2 Tablespoons red wine vinegar
MEDIUM

Directions: In a salad bowl, toss ingredients together, then chill in the refrigerator for at least two hours.

Caesar Salad
2 garlic cloves, crushed
½ teaspoon each of salt and pepper
1 Tablespoon lemon juice
1 hardboiled egg, peeled and thinly sliced
1/3 cup olive oil
1 head romaine lettuce, washed and torn into bite-sized pieces
½ cup grated parmesan cheese
1 cup onion & garlic croutons
MEDIUM

Directions: In a large salad bowl, mix garlic, salt, pepper, lemon juice and egg. Next, add olive oil and mix to combine. Place lettuce in the salad bowl and toss the salad. Lastly, add parmesan cheese and onion & garlic croutons. Serves Four.

"We call ourselves vegetarians, inside joke."-Edward Cullen

Broccoli Salad
1-2 bunches of broccoli
¾ cup raisins
½ cup red onions, chopped
12 slices of bacon, fried and crumbled
¾ cup of nuts (cashews, peanuts, or sunflower seeds)
Dressing
1 cup of mayonnaise
½ cup of sugar
2 Tablespoons of red wine vinegar
MEDIUM

Directions: Cut broccoli into small pieces, and place into bowl. Combine with nuts, raisins, onion, and bacon. Mix dressing ingredients and pour over broccoli mixture. Stir together. Chill for 1 to 2 hours.

Cobb Salad

A Full head of lettuce, shredded
1 hard boiled egg
Bacon, cooked and crumbled
Chicken, cooked and cubed
Roma Tomato, chopped finely
Avocado, pitted and cut up
Dressing
1/3 cup Vinegar
1 teaspoon salt
¼ teaspoon pepper
½ teaspoon dry mustard
½ teaspoon sugar
1/8 teaspoon garlic powder
2/3 cup of salad oil
¼ cup of blue cheese crumbled

Directions: Mix all ingredients in a bowl, chill for an hour, then serve.

"Charlie needs me. He's just all alone up there and can't cook at all." -Bella

Chief Swan Salad

Head of lettuce, washed, torn, and shredded
Red onion, diced
Green cucumber, sliced
Ham, cubed
Radishes, cut up
Tomatoes, diced
1 hard boiled egg, diced.
EASY
*Can also add cubed salami and bologna to your Chief's Salad.

Directions: Mix all ingredients in a bowl, add cubed salami or bologna if you desire.

Lobster Salad
Ice berg lettuce, cut
2 tomatoes, cut into wedges
Lobster meat
1 cup of chopped celery
2 hard boiled eggs,
½ cup of mayonnaise
2 teaspoon of lemon juice
1 teaspoon ketchup
½ teaspoon sugar
¼ teaspoon of salt
MEDIUM

Directions: Combine lobster, celery and eggs in a bowl. Mix the next five dressing ingredients together well, pour over lobster mixture. Top lobster mixture over a bed of lettuce. Place tomato wedges on the side.

Artichoke Cheese Squares
2 jars of marinated artichoke hearts
1 small onion chopped fine.
1 clove of garlic, chopped
4 eggs
¼ cup of bread crumbs
¼ teaspoon salt, pepper, oregano.
1/8 teaspoon liquid hot pepper
2 cups shredded sharp cheddar cheese
1 teaspoon of parsley, optional
MEDIUM

Directions: Mix all ingredients together and transfer into a greased 7x11 glass baking pan. Bake at 325 degrees for thirty minutes.

Bagel Bites
20 small (miniature bagels)
1 cup of mozzarella cheese, shredded
½ cup of pepperoni, cut finely
1 cup of pizza sauce

Salt and pepper to taste
Oregano or Italian seasoning to taste
EASY

Directions: Cut bagels in half and place bagels on a large baking sheet. Next, place the pizza sauce on each of the bagels and then add shredded cheese, and pepperoni slices. Add seasoning to taste and place in a 350 degree oven for 15 to 20 minutes or until toasty with cheese melted.

Get Out The Forks and Knives (Main Dishes)

Bella left Charlie a note on the table explaining again where to find dinner.

Stir Fry ala Swan
½ Tablespoon of vegetable oil
1 Tablespoon of sugar
1 pound of lean hamburger
2 teaspoons of minced garlic
1 medium onion, diced
1 medium head of cabbage shredded or cut into slightly larger than bite size pieces.
1 can (10 ¾ ounces) of tomato soup
1 can (8 ounces) of tomato sauce
¼ cup of water
1 Tablespoon of soy sauce and 1 teaspoon of salt (optional)
MEDIUM

Directions: In a skillet, over medium heat, add 1/2 Tablespoon of vegetable oil. Next, add 1 Tablespoon of sugar, the uncooked hamburger meat, diced onion, and minced garlic. With a spatula, break apart hamburger meat and cook uncovered over medium heat until hamburger meat is thoroughly cooked. Once the hamburger meat is browned, take off the stove top and remove the excess fat. Wash the skillet out with lukewarm water and place the cooked meat with garlic and onion back in the skillet and add the cabbage, tomato soup and tomato sauce (optional: may add salt and soy sauce). Cook covered over low heat until cabbage is tender, about 20 minutes. Makes 6 to 8 servings and can be complemented with white or brown rice.

Helpful Hint: To remove excess oil from hamburger meat, scoop hamburger meat over a plate lined with paper towels, this will absorb the excess fat.

"Charlie came home with a large catch."-Bella

Charlie's Catch of the day Crab Cakes
1 Egg
3 Tablespoons of mayonnaise
4 teaspoons of lemon juice
1/8 teaspoon of red pepper flakes
1 teaspoon of dried tarragon
1 Tablespoon of minced green onions
8 ounces of crabmeat
1 Tablespoon of butter
Round crackers, broken up into cracker crumbs
MEDIUM

Directions: In a medium bowl, whisk together the egg, mayonnaise, lemon juice, red pepper flakes, tarragon, and green onions. Gently stir in the crabmeat, and mix in cracker crumbs, adding as much as desired. Next, melt butter in a skillet over medium heat. Form crab patties and place in the skillet brown both sides until the patties are golden brown. Depending upon the size of the patties, makes about four crab cakes.

And so the lion fell in love with the lamb.

Lion and the Lamb Stew
2 ½ pounds of boneless lamb, cut into 1 ½ inch pieces
1/3 cup of flour
2 ½ teaspoons of salt
¼ teaspoon of pepper
¼ cup of butter

1 medium yellow onion, quartered
1 clove of garlic, minced
8 whole mushrooms
12 medium yellow onions
1 ¼ teaspoons of dried thyme leaves
2 springs of parsley
1 bay leaf
1 ½ cups of red wine
5 to 6 carrots, peeled
8 small new potatoes
Chopped parsley (optional)
HARD

Directions: Blot lamb with a paper towel, discard towel. Trim fat from lamb and cut into bite-size pieces. Next, combine flour, salt and pepper, coat the lamb evenly with the flour mixture. Reserve any excess flour. Melt butter in a dutch oven or large saucepan, add the floured lamb pieces, quartered onion, and garlic. Cook until lamb is browned on all sides, stirring frequently. Add remaining ingredients and bring to a boil. Reduce heat, cover, and simmer for about 1 hour, until lamb is tender.

There was fish marinating for dinner with salad and bread left over from the night before.

Harry's Famous Fish Fry
4 cups of cooked rice
About 2 pounds of fresh fish fillets
3-4 sprigs of green onions, sliced, including green parts
5-7 Fresh mushrooms
2 medium zucchini
2 cups   sauce, cooled slightly
Parchment paper or aluminum foil

Harry's secret sauce
1 can of chicken broth, 14.5 ounces
½ cup of dry white wine

¼ cup of cornstarch, mixed with ¼ cup of cold water
2 Tablespoons grated Swiss cheese
2 Tablespoons grated Parmesan cheese
HARD

Directions: In a medium sized sauce pan, heat chicken broth and wine, over high heat, stirring in approximately ½ of the cornstarch mixture, stir and cook until the mixture thickens, reduce heat to low, then add the seasonings. Taste to adjust flavor. Let cool slightly before assembling the fish packets. The assembly of the packets starts with an 18x15 inch sheet of parchment (or aluminum foil), folding in half to 9x15, placing ¼ of each of the ingredients, the rice, green onion, mushrooms, fish, other veggies, adding lemon juice to the top and Harry's secret sauce. Seal and place packets on a baking sheet in a 425 degree oven for 20 minutes.

"Charlie seemed suspicious when he came home and smelled the green peppers."-Bella

Bella thinks about Edward as she prepares Chicken Enchiladas for dinner.

Chicken Enchiladas
2 1/2 cups of tomato sauce
2 Tablespoons of oil
1 Tablespoon of cumin
3/4 teaspoon of chili powder
1/2 teaspoon of pepper
½ large green pepper, finely diced into bite size pieces
5-7 (Corn and flour tortillas)
MEDIUM

Directions: Combine ingredients in a medium size sauce pan and simmer for thirty minutes on medium heat.

Sauce
1 1/2 cups of enchilada Sauce
1 1/4 cups of stewed tomatoes
1/4 cup of chopped green chilies, drained
3 cups of shredded chicken
1 medium onion, finely diced
1 1/2 cups of stewed tomatoes, drained

3/4 cup of chopped green chilies, drained
1 teaspoon of chili powder
1 teaspoon of ground cumin
1/2 teaspoon of pepper

Directions: Combine and simmer for fifteen minutes. Brush inside of tortilla with two tablespoons of enchilada sauce and top each tortilla with 3 to 4 tablespoons of chicken mixture. Mix grated cheese, and place cheese inside of tortilla and roll up the tortilla. Next, place the tortilla roll, in a baking dish and pour the remaining enchilada sauce over the tortilla mixture, including the remaining cheese. Bake 20 to 25 minutes in a 350 degree oven.

"He was brave enough to take the first bite and he seemed to like the chicken enchiladas".-Bella talking about her dad Charlie

Cheese Enchiladas
1/4 cup chopped onion
1 Tablespoon butter
2 cups monterey jack cheese, shredded
1 pound of white cheddar cheese, shredded
2 Tablespoons of chopped black olives
2 tablespoons of finely diced jalapeno chilies
1 teaspoon of salt
12 corn tortillas
MEDIUM

Directions: Cook onion in butter until tender in a frying pan. In a separate skillet, fry tortillas in oil until soft, and drain excess oil. Add cheeses, olives, chilies, and seasonings to the tortillas and fold in half. Place in a greased shallow baking dish and bake at 350 degrees for 20 minutes, or until cheese has melted. Add Enchilada Sauce to taste.

"I hurried downstairs to take the potatoes out and put the steak in the broil."-Bella

Steak and Potatoes
1 beef brisket, 2 pounds
1 bottle of BBQ Sauce
1 Tablespoon of garlic powder
3 Tablespoons of paprika
2 teaspoons of brown sugar
2 teaspoons of onion powder
2 teaspoons of black pepper
2 teaspoons of chili powder
3 to 5 potatoes
MEDIUM

Directions: Rub seasoning on brisket and place in a crock pot; cover with BBQ sauce and cook on low for 8 hours with lid covered. Makes 4 to 6 servings. In a separate crock pot, may add washed potatoes for about four hours on high, or you may scrub a few potatoes, poke a few holes with a fork into the potatoes, wrap in aluminum foil. Place in a 350 degree oven for about an hour.

Cascade Mountain Mashed Potatoes
3 pounds of potatoes, peeled and cut into 1 ½ inch pieces
¾ cup of milk
1 can (7 ounces) of chipotle pepper
Salt and pepper to taste
MEDIUM

Directions: Cut and peel potatoes and place in a large stockpot and cover with water, bringing to a boil. Cook potatoes until tender, then drain. Add milk and chipotle sauce to potatoes and mash. Season with salt and pepper. Makes 6 to 8 servings.

Bella's Instant Mashed Potatoes
4 cups chopped white potatoes
¼ cup low-fat milk
Minced garlic
2 Tablespoon of cream cheese or grated cheddar cheese
½ teaspoon of salt

1/8 teaspoon of pepper
MEDIUM

Directions: Cut and peel potatoes and place in a saucepan with water. Bring to a boil, and reduce the heat to low. Cook for 20 minutes, or until soft. Once the potatoes are cooked, drain the water and add milk, garlic, cream cheese, salt and pepper. Mash the ingredients with an electric mixer. Serve warm.

Pot Roast with vegetables
4-5lbs Pot roast(chuck, round, shoulder or rump roast)
flour
Salt
pepper
1 teaspoon of sugar
1/2 cup water
1 package Onion Soup mix
5-7 mini carrots
4-5 pearl sized onions
5-7 whole new small potatoes
MEDIUM

Directions: Place roast in a deep pot with a lid cover. Dredge roast with flour, salt, pepper and sugar (for browning) Grease pan lightly. Over high heat, brown roast well on all sides. Will take about 30 minutes. Once dark brown, place rack under the roast. Add 1/2 cup of water and package of onion soup mix. Cover Lower heat and cook very slowly for 2 hrs. Next, add small whole potatoes, pearl sized onions, and small carrots. Coat veggies with the onion soup mix in the pot and continue cooking for an additional hour. Serves 8 to 10.

Irritated Grizzly Bear Steaks
Beef tri-tip, 2 pounds
½ teaspoon of chili powder
½ teaspoon of paprika
½ teaspoon of cumin

¼ teaspoon of garlic powder and onion powder
MEDIUM

Directions: Rub seasonings on tri tip and refrigerate until ready to grill. On a barbeque grill, roast over medium heat, turning occasionally, about 35 minutes. Carve tri-tip into slices. Makes 4 to 6 servings.

"What's for dinner?"-Charlie (Charlie asked Bella warily, partially due to the fact, according to Bella that her mother was an imaginative cook, her experiments however, weren't always edible.)

Charlie's Dinner in a Skillet
1 package of hot dogs, sliced into ¼ inch pieces
4 potatoes, peeled and cubed
1 green pepper, sliced
¼ cup of red onion, diced
Vegetable or olive oil
EASY

Directions: in a skillet, on medium heat, add 2-3 tablespoons of oil. When warm, add the hot dogs, potatoes, green pepper, and onion. Sautee the ingredients and cook until hot dogs are browned and potatoes are cooked. May add 2-3 tablespoons of water and can reduce heat, if necessary.

Arizona Corn Bake
1 pound of ground beef
2 cans (14.5 ounces each) of Canned Diced Tomatoes
1 can (15 ounces) of Canned Corn, drained
1 Tablespoon of Chili Powder
1 Package of Corn Muffin Mix (may need an egg)
EASY

Directions: In a skillet, brown meat; drain. Next, add the canned tomatoes and corn as well as chili powder. Season to taste with salt and pepper. Pour into a 2-quart baking dish. Prepare the muffin mix according to the package directions. Spread the muffin mixture evenly over the cooked meat and bake at 400 degree for 25 minutes or until golden.

"The closest edible Mexican food was probably in Southern, California."-Bella

Taco Soup

1 ½ pounds of hamburger (browned and drained, salt and pepper to taste as well as onion flakes, about 1 Tbs.)
1 can corn, not drained
1 can kidney beans, juice as well
1 large can of Mexican or Italian stewed tomatoes
1 can of tomato soup
1 package of taco seasoning mix
EASY

Directions: cook the hamburger meat until browned with a little seasoning and drain. In a large pot, add can of corn, kidney beans, stewed tomatoes, can of tomato soup, and 1 can of water as well as the taco seasoning mix. Combine all of the ingredients along with the cooked hamburger meat and simmer for 45 minutes.

Beef Stew

4 Tablespoons oil
1 cup burgundy wine
1 clove garlic, crushed
1 (10 oz.) can beef consommé
2 large onions, sliced
1 (10 oz.) package frozen artichoke hearts
1 Tablespoons butter
1 1/2 teaspoons salt
1/4 teaspoon pepper
18 fresh mushrooms, halved
2 1/2 lb. stew beef
1/2 teaspoon dill weed
Refrigerated biscuit dough
EASY

Directions: brown beef in oil; add onions, garlic, salt, and pepper. In a pot, place beef mixture as well as dill weed, wine and consommé. Cover tightly and simmer for 1 1/2 hours or until tender. Sauté artichokes and mushrooms in butter and add to meat; simmer an additional 20 minutes. Remove from heat. Top with biscuits and brush biscuits with butter and sprinkle with parmesan cheese.

"Mom is an unpredictable cook."-Bella talking about her mother

South of the Phoenix Border Casserole
1 pound of lean beef
½ cup of chopped yellow or white onion
2 (8 ounce) cans of tomato sauce
1 Tablespoon of chili powder
1 teaspoon of salt
1 dozen flour or corn tortillas
Cheddar cheese grated
MEDIUM

Directions: Brown meat and onions in a skilled and cook until meat is cooked thoroughly. Stir in the tomato sauce and seasonings. Alternate layers of meat and tortillas and cheese and place in a glass casserole dish. Bake for 20 minutes in a 325 degree oven.

"Forks was literally, my personal hell on earth."-Bella

You'll need to Get Out the Forks Baked Beans
2 Cups of Navy Beans
½ pound of cooked bacon
1 onion, finely diced
3 Tablespoons of molasses
2 teaspoons of salt
¼ teaspoon black pepper, ground
¼ teaspoon dry mustard
½ cup of ketchup
1 Tablespoon of Worcestershire sauce
¼ cup of brown sugar
MEDIUM

Directions: Soak the navy beans overnight in cold water. The next day, use the same water and simmer the beans in a pot for about 1 hour. Arrange beans in a bean pot or a casserole dish, placing a portion of the beans in the bottom of the dish and then layering them with bacon and onion. Next, in a saucepan, combine the molasses, salt and pepper, ketchup, mustard, brown sugar and Worcestershire sauce. Mix and bring the mixture to a boil and then pour over the beans. Cover the casserole dish and bake for three hours in a 325 degree oven. Cook until beans are tender, add more liquid if needed.

Melt in your Mouth Coq au Vin
2 chicken breasts, split
Salt and pepper to taste
1/3 cup butter
1 ½ cups sliced fresh mushrooms
¼ cup white Burgundy wine
2 Tablespoons of orange juice
1 teaspoon grated orange rind
1 10 ½ ounce cream of chicken soup
MEDIUM

Directions: remove skin and bones from chicken breasts, and wash in water. Pat dry. Sprinkle chicken with salt and pepper. Heat butter in a skillet and brown chicken on both sides. Add mushrooms and sauté mushrooms. Add remaining ingredients and simmer until chicken is cooked, about twenty minutes. Serve with white rice.

Chow Bella

"Just eat Bella."-Edward

Mushroom Ravioli

10 ounces mushroom ravioli, or cheese filled ravioli
2 tablespoons of olive oil
2 ounces of shiitake mushrooms, sliced
4 ounces white mushrooms, sliced
1 clove of garlic, minced
¼ cup brandy
1 cup heavy cream
½ teaspoon of nutmeg
Salt and pepper
½ cup of grated Parmesan cheese

EASY

Directions: Prepare ravioli according to package directions, drain. Next, over medium heat, pour olive oil in a skillet, cook mushrooms until tender and add garlic. Add brandy and cook for 2 minutes. Slowly, stir in heavy cream and bring to a simmer. Season with nutmeg, salt and pepper. When cream has thickened, stir in ¼ cup of parmesan cheese. Then, stir in cooked ravioli and gently simmer for 1-2 minutes. Serve with parmesan, garlic bread and salad. Makes 2 servings.

Tallerina

3 Tablespoons shortening
1 onion, minced
1 lb. ground round
1 cans tomato soup
1 15 oz. can tomato sauce
1 cup cold water

2 Tablespoons salt
2 cups uncooked broad egg noodles
2 cups of whole grain canned corn
1 can ripe pitted olives
1 cup grated cheddar cheese
1 can mushrooms
MEDIUM

Directions: Melt shortening in a large pot, add onions and cook until brown. Next, add meat and brown; then add tomato soup, tomato sauce, noodles, water, and salt. Cover and cook over low heat for 10 minutes. Remove pot from stove and add corn, mushrooms, and part of the cheddar cheese and mix. Pour entire mixture into a baking dish; cover with remaining cheese and bake at 350 degrees for 50 minutes.

Zucchini Relleno
1 ¼ pounds of zucchini, cubed
4 eggs
½ cup of milk
1 pound of jack cheese, cubed
2 teaspoon of baking powder
3 Tablespoons of Flour
2 Tablespoons of Parsley Flakes
1 Small can of diced Green Chilies
½ cube of Butter or Margarine
½ teaspoon of dry bread crumbs
Salt and pepper to taste
Cooking spray
MEDIUM

Directions: Boil squash for five mines, then drain and cool. Next, blend eggs, milk and all of the dry ingredients. Spray a 9x9 inch pan with cooking spray and then sprinkle with bread crumbs. Layer the squash, cheese and chilies. Pour liquid mixture over the squash with cut up butter or margarine pieces. Bake at 350 degrees for 35 minutes or until set. Cut into squares and serve as an appetizer.

Pasta with Creamy Garlic and Walnut Sauce
1 ½ cups of heavy cream
1 cup of walnuts
¾ cup of shredded romano cheese
2 garlic cloves, peeled
1 teaspoon of salt
½ teaspoon of ground black pepper
1 pound of bow tie shaped pasta
EASY

Directions: place cream, walnuts, cheese, salt and pepper and garlic into a food processor and blend until mixture is smooth. Cook pasta according to the package directions, and drain. Toss pasta with the sauce and return to a pan to heat the sauce. May garnish with cilantro and additional walnuts. *candied walnuts make the pasta have a little sweet kick.

Veal Scaloppini
2 ½ pounds of boned Veal Shoulder
½ cup cups of flour
2 teaspoons of salt
¼ teaspoon of pepper
½ cup of minced onion
½ cup of vegetable oil
¾ cup of canned whole or sliced fresh mushrooms
1 ¾ cup of tomato juice or strained tomatoes
1 teaspoon of sugar
HARD

Directions: Cut veal into 1 ½ inch cubes. Roll the cubes lightly in flour combined with ½ teaspoon of salt and ½ teaspoon of pepper (or a dash of salt and pepper, to taste). Sauté minced onion in a skillet using the hot vegetable oil. Once the minced onion is browned, take out of the skillet and place it in a 2 quart casserole dish. Next, place floured veal in the same skillet and brown on all sides. Add mushrooms, tomatoes, sugar, remaining 1 ½ teaspoons salt and 1/8 teaspoon pepper. Cover and bake in the oven at 350 degrees for 1 ½ hours or until tender.

Chicken Cacciatore
1- 3 pound whole fryer chicken, cut into pieces and washed
½ cup of oil
Garlic salt to taste
2 Tablespoons of chopped parsley
1 clove of garlic
Pinch of thyme
2 leaves of sage
1 sprig of rosemary
1 small can of Italian stewed tomatoes, chopped
1 small can of tomato sauce
1 can of button mushroom, drain
HARD

Directions: Cut and wash chicken pieces. In a deep frying pan, place oil and cut pieces of chicken, sprinkle with garlic salt and cook until chicken has browned. Once the chicken has browned, add the herbs and spices as well as the tomato sauce, chopped tomatoes, and mushrooms. Cook on high heat for thirty minutes.

Create Your Own Perfect Pizza
English Muffins
Pizza or spaghetti sauce
Mozzarella cheese
Pineapple chunks
Pepperoni
Black olives
Green pepper
Fresh sliced mushrooms
EASY

Directions: Slice all of the ingredients into bite sized pieces. Grate the mozzarella cheese and place the pizza or spaghetti sauce on an English muffin. After the sauce is on the muffin, add cheese and your favorite toppings. Place the pizza on a cookie sheet and bake at 350 degrees for 6 minutes or until cheese is melted.

"People can't smell blood."-Edward Cullen

Pasta with Broccoli and Artichokes
1 pound bow tie pasta
Broccoli halved
Pepperoni, cut into 1 inch slivers
Marinated artichoke hearts, diced
½ cup of sun dried tomatoes
3 green onions, chopped
1 Tablespoon of red-wine vinegar
¼ teaspoon salt
¼ teaspoon pepper
¼ cup of parmesan cheese
MEDIUM

    Directions: In a pot, cook pasta in lightly salted water for 10 minutes, or until bow tie pasta is tender. Add broccoli to boiling water in the last five minutes of cooking, then drain. Add the cooked pasta to a bowl and add the other ingredients, and toss. Serve hot or cold. Parmesan cheese as a topping is optional.

Spaghettini Primavera
4 Tablespoons of olive oil
1 pound of sweet Italian sausage
2 dried hot chili peppers
1 (28 ounce) can of Italian plum tomatoes, drained and diced
1 cup of finely minced parsley
2 large garlic cloves, minced
3 red bell peppers, peeled, seeded and thinly sliced
1 sprig of fresh oregano or 1 teaspoon of dried oregano
Salt and pepper to taste
¾ pound of spaghettini
3 Tablespoons of finely minced parsley (as garnish, optional)
3 Tablespoons of Parmesan cheese
MEDIUM

    Directions: Heat two tablespoons of olive oil in a large skillet over medium heat. Add sausage, cover and cook until browned on all sides. This will take about twenty or so minutes. Next, in the same skillet, add more oil and heat on medium to high heat the chili peppers and sauté until skins turn black. Take the chili peppers out of the heat once they are cooked and then add the tomatoes, parsley and garlic to the skillet and bring to a simmer.

Reduce the heat and add the red pepper, oregano and salt and pepper to taste. Cover and simmer for about 10 minutes. Cook the spaghettini according to package directions and drain the water. Slice the sausage and add to a large bowl all of the ingredients, discard chili peppers. Top with a sprig of parsley (as garnish) and sprinkle with parmesan cheese. May serve with garlic or toasted french bread.

"Charlie seemed absentminded at dinner."-Bella

"It was fun to watch as he slowly began trusting me in the kitchen."-Bella

Bells' Lasagna
1 container, 15 ounces of ricotta cheese
1 egg
1 package, 8 ounces of shredded mozzarella cheese, and 1/3 cup parmesan cheese
1 jar, 28 ounces of Spaghetti Sauce
1 can of tomato sauce, 8 ounces
½ of a 16 ounce box of uncooked lasagna noodles.
Optional: 1 box of frozen chopped spinach, 1 cup of sliced mushrooms, or 1 cup shredded zucchini
Spices to season with: basil, oregano, garlic, parsley, and fenugreek.
HARD

Directions: Preheat oven to 350 degrees. Combine ricotta cheese, egg, and parmesan-mozzarella cheese combination as well as the seasonings in a bowl, mix well. Next, spray the bottom of a 9x13 inch pan and place part of the cooked lasagna noodles. Once the noodles are in the pan, start layering with the ricotta mixture, spaghetti sauce, tomato sauce, and remaining noodles. (May add optional ingredients at this time as well). Cover with aluminum foil and bake for 75 minutes in a 350 degree oven. Allow to cool 10 to 15 minutes before serving.

"He looks at you like you're something to eat."-Mike

Easy Chicken Swan Parmesan
4 boneless chicken breast, washed and pounded to ½ inch in thickness (or pre purchase thin chicken filets)
1 Egg
½ cup of milk
Italian Seasoned Bread Crumbs
8 slices of mozzarella cheese
1 jar of Spaghetti Sauce (any flavor)
Parmesan cheese to taste
Salt and pepper to taste
MEDIUM

Directions: Dip washed chicken breasts into the egg and milk mixture. The egg and milk mixture needs to be slightly mixed with a fork, add a dash of salt and pepper the egg/milk mixture. Once dipped in the egg/milk mixture, then dip the chicken breasts into the bread crumbs. In a glass baking dish, place the chicken and pour 1 jar of your favorite spaghetti sauce over the chicken. Next, place mozzarella slices and parmesan cheese and bake for thirty minutes in a 350 degree oven. Make sure chicken is no longer pink in the middle, by taking out of the oven and with a fork and knife, cutting a center piece to check for doneness. May serve with garlic bread and a salad or a side of green beans.

Bite at Twilight (Desserts)

Time for Tea Cake Cookies
(a London pre-vampire Carlisle Cookie)
1/2 cup of margarine
3/4 cup of confectioner's sugar (powdered sugar)
1 Tablespoon of vanilla extract
1 1/2 cups of flour
1/8 teaspoon of salt
Food coloring-optional
Chocolate pieces, peanut butter chips, nuts, cherries.
MEDIUM

Mix together:
1 cup of confectioner's sugar
3 1/2 Tablespoons milk
1 teaspoon of vanilla extract
Food coloring-optional

Directions: Heat oven to 350 degrees. Thoroughly mix together margarine, vanilla, sugar, and three drops of food coloring (any color). Add flour and salt and work until dough can hold together. Mold dough by Tablespoonfuls around a few chocolate pieces, nuts, or cherries. Place cookie dough on a baking sheet approximately 1 inch apart for 10 minutes or until light brown.
Once the cookies are cool, dip tops of cookies into Icing. Decorate cookies with colored sugar, sprinkles, candies, or coconut. Yields 25 cookies.

"Why the traffic jam last night?"

Why the Traffic Jam Cookies
2 ½ cups of all-purpose flour
½ teaspoon of baking powder
1 cup margarine or butter, softened
1 egg
1 cup of white sugar
2 teaspoons of vanilla extract

1 cup of your favorite flavor of fruit jam
Makes 4 dozen cookies
MEDIUM

Directions: Preheat the oven to 300 degrees. In a bowl, combine flour and baking powder. Mix well and set aside. Next, in a medium sized bowl, cream butter/margarine and sugar, egg, and vanilla extract. Beat with an electric mixer until smooth. Add the flour mixture and blend on low speed until combined. Roll the dough into 1 inch balls and place on a baking sheet, approximately 1 inch apart. With your thumb, press down the center of the dough balls and shape the ball to form a circle in the middle of the ball. Place a small amount of jam in the center of the dough ball, about ½ of a teaspoon of jam. Bake 20 minutes in a 300 degree oven until golden brown.

Red Velvet Cake
4 Tablespoons cocoa powder
1 ounce liquid red food coloring
3/4 cup of water
1 yellow cake mix, with pudding in the mix
4 eggs
1 teaspoon vanilla extract
1 teaspoon of butter
4 Tablespoons of buttermilk
1 Tablespoon of white vinegar
MEDIUM

Directions: Preheat oven to 325 degrees. Mix cocoa powder, red food coloring and part of the water to form a paste. Next, add all of the other ingredients, omitting the white vinegar. Blend for 2 ½ to 3 minutes with a mixer until on medium speed. Then add the vinegar and mix with a spatula and then pour the batter into a bunt or round cake pan and bake for approximately 35 minutes. Can make this recipe into cupcakes as well. Adorn each cupcake or the entire Red Velvet Cake with various miniature die cast Cullen cars such as Carlisle's Mercedes S55 AMG, Rosalie's red BMW M3, Edward's silver, Volvo S60R, Alice's yellow Porsche 911 Turbo, or Emmett's Jeep Wrangler . Could also add a replica of Bella's red Chevy pickup truck.

Jasper Cookie Bars

1/2 cup margarine or butter
1 1/2 cups gram cracker crumbs
1 (14 ounce) can sweetened condensed milk
1 (6 ounce) package of semi-sweet or milk chocolate chips
1 1/3 cup of coconut flakes
1 cup of chopped walnuts
MEDIUM

Directions: Preheat the oven to 350 degrees. Melt butter in the microwave and add gram cracker crumbs to the melted butter. Next, in a 13x9 inch baking pan, place gram cracker crumb mixture and press down with a fork, covering the bottom of the pan. P   our a can of sweetened condensed milk on top of gram cracker crumb mixture. Then sprinkle the remaining ingredients of chocolate chips, nuts, and coconut flakes and bake for 25 minutes. Once cooled, cut into bite size squares. Creates a delicious concoction of chocolate and coconut. You may add peanut butter chips, or white chocolate chips to the recipe if you desire.

Forbidden Love Coconut Lemon Crumb Squares
(Sinfully delicious)

1 ¾ cups of Graham cracker crumbs
½ cup granulated sugar
¾ cup margarine, melted
¾ cup all-purpose flour
½ cup of coconut
MEDIUM

Filling
½ cup of granulated sugar
1 egg
1 cup of lemon juice, plus ¼ teaspoon of lemon rind
½ coconut

Directions: Melt the margarine and pour over the first ingredients. Combine in a large bowl and work together until crumbly. Press the mixture into an not greased 9x9 inch pan and set aside. Next, place filling ingredients in a pot on low heat, stirring until thickened. Pour filling over bottom layer. Cook for 25 minutes in a 350 degree oven. Depending on the size you cut for the squares, makes approximately 30 squares.

Perfect for the Prom Bella's Bonbons
1/4 cup melted butter
1 can sweetened condensed milk
1 lb. powdered sugar
1 package coconut
1 package chocolate chips
1/2 cube Parowax

Directions: Combine butter, milk, sugar and coconut. Chill at least 30 minutes. Form into small balls and chill again. Melt chocolate chips and wax over hot water. Dip balls into chocolate mixture quickly and remove with fork. Put on waxed paper to cool. Makes 2 dozen bonbons.

Sink Your Teeth into Peanut Butter Pie
(Don't forget the milk)
1 carton frozen whipped topping (8 ounces)
1 ready made graham cracker crust
½ cup strawberry jelly
1 cup cold milk
1 package instant vanilla pudding mix
½ cup of creamy peanut butter

Directions: Spread 1 cup of the whipped topping over the bottom of the crust. Drop jelly by the tablespoonfuls onto whipped topping. In a bowl, whisk milk and pudding mix until thickened. Add peanut better; mix well. Then, fold in the leftover whipped topping, spread over the jelly. Allow to harden in the freezer for at least 2 hours. Serves 6-8.

"Everyone enjoys different flavors…chocolate ice cream, strawberry, sorry about the food analogy."-Bella speaking to her vampire boyfriend Edward

Everyone Enjoys Different Flavors Sundae
Chocolate, Vanilla or Strawberry ice cream
Hot Fudge topping
Blanched almonds (optional)
Fresh, seasonal strawberries, blackberries, blueberries
Maraschino cherries on top
Whipped cream

Directions: Heat fudge in either a saucepan or in the microwave (follow heating instructions on label). Spoon hot fudge onto scooped ice cream. Make your sundae complete with fresh toppings such as slivered almonds, berries, whipped cream, and cherries.

"I like the night." –Bella

"Without the dark, we'd never see the stars."-Bella

Starry Night Cake
1- 1/4 cups all-purpose flour
1 cup granulated sugar
1- 1/2 teaspoons baking powder
1/2 teaspoon salt
3/4 cup of milk
1/3 cup of shortening
1 egg
1 teaspoon vanilla extract
Star Cookie cutter (or handmade star stencil)
Powdered sugar

Directions: Preheat oven to 350 degrees. Grease and flour two 9-inch round pans. In a mixing bowl, add sugar, milk, shortening, egg, and vanilla extract. Blend the ingredients on medium speed for 2 minutes, slowly adding the flour, baking powder, and salt. Continue to blend for 3 more minutes scraping the sides of the bowl with a spatula.
Once the cake batter is smooth, pour an equal amount of cake batter into each floured round pan. Bake 35 to 40 minutes at 350 degrees on center rack. Once cake is cooled, place the star stencil on top. With a sifter, sift

powdered sugar over the stencil covering thoroughly. Gently remove stencil to reveal star shape. Repeat several times to create starry night.

Twilight Chocolate Cake

2-1/4 cups all-purpose flour
1-2/3 cups granulated sugar
2/3 cup cocoa
1-1/4 teaspoons baking soda
1 teaspoon salt
1/4 teaspoon baking powder
1-1/4 cups water
3/4 cup shortening
2 eggs
1 teaspoon vanilla extract

Directions: Preheat oven to 350 degrees. Grease and flour two 9-inch round layer pans. Place all ingredients into a large bowl and blend with an electric mixer on low speed for a minute. Increase to high speed and mix an additional 3 minutes. Take a spatula and scrape the sides and bottom of bowl, make sure all of the ingredients have been mixed well. Pour the batter into the two greased and floured pans.
 Bake for 30-35 minutes or until tooth pick inserted in center comes out clean. Cool. Top with Midnight frosting.

Midnight Frosting

1/2 cup sugar
1/4 cup corn syrup
2 Tablespoons water
2 egg whites
1 teaspoon vanilla extract

Directions: Place sugar, syrup and water in a saucepan. Cover the saucepan, and boil over medium heat. As the mixture boils, beat egg whites until stiff. Pour mixture from saucepan slowly into egg whites, beating constantly with electric mixer on medium speed. Add vanilla extract while beating.

"I did once, on a dare" – Bella (eat dirt that is).

Dare to Eat Dirt Pie
Foil Cupcake liners
Chocolate cookies
Chocolate pudding
Gummy worm candies

Directions: Crush cookies in a plastic bag until they are crumbs. Next, spoon chocolate pudding into a cupcake tin. On top of the chocolate pudding, layer with cookie crumbs and gummy worms. May use store bought chocolate pudding or try Dare to Eat Mud Chocolate pudding recipe.

Dare to Eat Mud Chocolate Pudding
1/3 cup sugar
2 tablespoons cornstarch
¼ cup of unsweetened cocoa powder
1/8 teaspoon salt
2 cups milk
2 egg yolks, slightly beaten
4 ounces of semi-sweet chocolate chips
2 tablespoons butter
2 teaspoons vanilla extract

Directions: Blend sugar, cornstarch, unsweetened cocoa powder and salt in a 2-quart saucepan. Combine milk and egg yolks; gradually stir into sugar mixture, and slowly add in the semi-sweet chocolate chips. Cook over medium heat, stirring constantly, until it thickens. Boil and stir 1 minute. Remove from heat, stir in butter and vanilla. Serves 4.

Bella mentions Edwards' eyes being the color of butterscotch.

Butterscotch Bars
1 cup of all-purpose flour

6-Tablespoons of brown sugar
1/8 teaspoon of salt
½ cup of butter or margarine
6 ounce package (1/2 of a package) of butterscotch chips
1-Tablespoon of Corn syrup
1-Tablespoon of Water
2-Tablespoons of butter or margarine
1/8 teaspoon of salt
2/3 cup of walnuts, chopped (optional)

Directions: In a bowl, stir together flour, brown sugar, salt and margarine or butter. Next, press the crumbled mixture into a not greased 9x9 inch pan. Bake in a 375 degree oven for 10 minutes. Next, combine the remaining five ingredients into a saucepan on low heat. Melt mixture and then add the walnuts, if desired. Pour the mixture over the first layer and place back into a 375 degree oven for 8 minutes. Once cooled, cut into squares. Makes approximately 25 Butterscotch bars.

Butterscotch Eyes
1 package Butterscotch Instant Pudding
2 cups applesauce
½ teaspoon ground cinnamon
1 cup thawed cool whip
1 cup of Honey Teddy Grahams

Directions: Mix dry pudding, add applesauce and cinnamon in medium bowl with a wire whisk for 2 minutes or until well blended. Gently stir in whipped topping. Alternate butterscotch mixture and cool whip in parfait glasses. Garnish edges with teddy grahams.
Makes 4 servings.

Love at First Bite Cupcakes
24 baked cupcakes (bake according to package directions)-Chocolate Cake Mix
24 Nutter-butter (name brand) cookies
Chocolate Frosting
Vanilla Frosting
Tube of chocolate, green, and red decorator's icing.

Directions: frost cupcakes with the chocolate frosting. Ice the entire Nutter-Butter cookie with white frosting and use decorator's icing to draw a vampire expression on each cookie. Place vampire cookie in the middle of the cupcake. Makes 24 Love at First Bite Cupcakes.

Vampire Cupcakes
1 package of chocolate cake mix
1 can of chocolate frosting
Cup cake liners
Tube of red decorators icing
Plastic vampire teeth

Directions: follow the chocolate cake mix directions and bake cupcakes in cupcake tins. Once cooled, frost with chocolate frosting, and add plastic vampire teeth and use red decorators icing to resemble blood dripping from teeth.

Vampire Bites
Red peanut MnM candies
Vanilla chocolate chips, 8 oz. package
2 cups pretzel twists (optional)
Wax paper

Directions: line a cookie sheet with waxed paper. Melt vanilla chips in microwave, about one minute. Pour melted chips onto waxed paper and spread with a spatula. Next, add red peanut mnm's and pretzel twists. Once cooled, break off into tiny pieces.

"Oh, she does smell good!"-Alice

Vampire Bite Bars
Graham crackers
1 cup brown sugar
½ cup butter
½ cup of milk
1 1/3 cups of graham cracker crumbs
1 cup of chopped walnuts

1 cup of coconut
¼ cup dried cherries.

    Directions: Line a 9x9 inch pan with whole graham crackers. In a saucepan, combine sugar, butter, and milk. Bring to a boil, simmer for about 2 minutes. Next, add cracker crumbs, nuts, coconut and cherries, mix well. Pour over the whole graham crackers and allow cooling. Let stand overnight. May add vanilla icing to top. Cut and serve squares.

Rocky Road Brownies
1 ¾ cups of granulated sugar
¾ cup of butter, softened
3 large eggs
2 teaspoons of vanilla extract
4 squares of unsweetened chocolate, melted and cooled
1/4 teaspoon of salt
½ cup of cocoa powder
¾ cup of flour
12 marshmallows
1 cup of finely chopped walnuts
1 cup of milk chocolate chips

    Directions: Heat oven to 350 degrees. Grease and flour a 9x13 inch pan, set aside. With an electric mixer on medium speed, cream sugars and butter until fluffy, then add the eggs and mix an additional 1 to 2 minutes. Then add in the chocolate, vanilla extract, cocoa, flour and salt. Once mixed, stir in the chocolate chips and walnuts. In a greased pan, lay marshmallows and spoon batter over the marshmallows. Bake at 350 degrees in the center rack for 25 minutes. Once cooled, cut into squares and may wrap them individually in waxed paper or cling wrap.

Get out the Forks Lemon Pie
Ready Made graham cracker crust
1 (3 ounce) package lemon flavored Jell-O
1 cup boiling water
½ block soft tofu
4 ounces of light whipped topping

1 Tablespoon of fresh lemon juice
1 teaspoon of lemon rind.

Directions: Dissolve the Jell-O in boiling water and cool. Add the tofu and blend with an electric mixer. Fold in the cool whip and add the lemon juice and rind. Pour into graham cracker shell and refrigerate until set. *This is a good substitute for lemon meringue pie if you are watching the calories.

Bella picks up an apple and states her curiosity to Edward turning the apple around in her hands and asking him what would he do if someone dared him to eat food?

Apple Cider Cheese Fondue
4 cups of shredded sharp cheddar cheese
1 ½ Tablespoons of cornstarch
1 ¼ cup of apple cider
¼ of a teaspoon of lemon juice
¼ of a teaspoon of salt
1/8 of a teaspoon of cinnamon
1/8 of a teaspoon of nutmeg

Directions: In a medium sized saucepan, over medium heat, warm cider and lemon juice until simmering. Next, toss cheese and cornstarch together and one handful at a time, place into the simmering apple cider mixture, stirring constantly. Stir in remaining spices. Cover over low heat until thickened. Transfer to a fondue pot to keep warm. May dip toasted bread, sliced cooked sausage, or apple slices, in fondue.

Apple of My Eye Pie
5-6 golden delicious apples, thinly sliced, removing seeds and apple skins
2 Tablespoons of lemon juice
1/3 cup of apple sauce
1/3 cup light brown sugar
1/3 cup of granulated sugar
1 teaspoon cinnamon

3 –9" ready to bake rolled dough pie crusts

1 egg white- beaten
2 tablespoons sugar- large crystal

Directions: Preheat oven to 450 degrees.
Mix apples, lemon juice, apple sauce, brown sugar, sugar and cinnamon and set aside. Grease muffin pan. Roll out dough and cut 12, 4-inch circles and 12, 3-inch circles out of the dough. Place the 4-inch in each muffin cup and fill with apple mixture. Top each mini-pie with a 3-inch circle and press edges together. Cut 4 slits in each pie top. Brush each pie with the egg white and sprinkle with sugar. Bake for 15-18 minutes, or until golden brown. Let cool before removing from muffin pan.
Makes 12 servings.

Apple Cider Spice
12 broken cinnamon sticks
¼ cup of whole cloves
¼ cup of allspice berries
1 teaspoon of nutmeg
Grated rind of 2 oranges
2 lemons
2 tangerines

Directions: Combine the ingredients and use one teaspoon of the mixture per mug of cider. Simmer the cider with the spices for ten minutes, then strain before serving.

Hot Mulled Apple Cider
½ cup of brown sugar
¼ teaspoon of salt
2 quarts cider
1 teaspoon of whole cloves
1 cinnamon stick

Directions: Combine brown sugar, salt, and cider. Add spices and slowly bring to a boil in a pot and then simmer uncovered, about twenty minutes. Remove the spices and serve warm.

Chunky Applesauce
9 cups of sliced apples
½ cup of apple cider
1 Tablespoon of lemon juice

½ cup of sugar
1/8 teaspoon of salt
½ teaspoon of nutmeg

Directions: Combine the apples, cider, and lemon juice in a saucepan, about a 3 quart saucepan. Bring to a boil over medium heat and simmer until apples are tender, about 15 to 20 minutes. Next, add sugar, salt and nutmeg and cook for a minute or so longer. Separate the apples into chunks. Can add cream and cinnamon to top of apple chunks.

Fried Apples
6 apples
¼ cup of butter
Brown sugar

Directions: Quarter and core the apples, but do not peel. Melt butter in a frying pan and place the apples in the pan. Sprinkle with brown sugar and cook with a little bit of water slowly. Wait until they are tender.

Apple Bread
¾ cup of vegetable oil
1 cup brown sugar
2 eggs
1 ½ cups chopped apple
¼ cup chopped walnuts
1 Tbs. lemon zest
1 ½ cups of flour
1 teaspoon cinnamon
½ teaspoon nutmeg
1 teaspoon baking soda
¼ teaspoon salt

Directions: Mix all ingredients and pour into a loaf pan. Bake at 350 degrees for 55 minutes, or until toothpick inserted comes out clean.

I Dare You American Apple Crisp
5 medium apples, sliced thin, Pippin or Granny Smith variety
½ cup yellow cake mix
¼ cup sugar and cinnamon combination
¼ cup melted butter

Directions: place sliced apples in a glass cooking dish, sprinkle in cake mix, as well as cinnamon sugar mixture. Pour melted margarine over the mixture. Bake for 25 minutes at 400 degrees.

An apple a day, hopefully won't keep Edward away.

Blushing Bella Apples
2 Red Baking Apples
¼ cup of Butter
2 Tablespoons of Flour
1 Teaspoon of Cinnamon
½ cup of Brown Sugar
¼ cup of Chopped Pecans

Directions: Preheat the oven to 400 degrees (reduce heat when ready to place apples in the oven). Core the apples and place the apples in a baking dish. Melt the butter and then stir in the flour, cinnamon, and brown sugar. Spoon the brown sugar mixture into the center of the cored apples. Sprinkle with chopped pecans (optional). Bake at 350 degrees for 30 minutes or until tender.

Werewolf Chow
9 cups of Chex Cereal, Rice
¼ cup of butter or margarine
1 cup of chocolate chips, semisweet
Or a combination of ½ cup of chocolate chips and ½ cup of peanut butter chips
½ cup of smooth peanut butter, not crunchy
1 teaspoon of vanilla extract
1 ½ cups of powdered sugar

Directions: In a large zip lock bag place the cereal. Next, microwave the chocolate chips, peanut butter and butter or margarine for about one minute. If the mixture hasn't melted, stir and place in microwave another 20-30 seconds. Once melted, stir in the vanilla extract. Pour the chocolate chip peanut butter mixture over the chex cereal and add the powdered sugar and shake. You may place mixture on waxed paper to spread the mixture out for cooling purposes. Place in a bowl, such as a brand new dog bowl. May add a sugar cookie bone shaped cookie to top of werewolf chow.

Too Hot to Handle
8 quarts of plain popped popcorn
1 cup butter or margarine
½ cup light corn syrup
1 package of red-hot candies.

Directions: Place popcorn in a large bowl and set aside. In a saucepan, combine butter, corn syrup and red hot candies, bring to a boil over medium heat stirring constantly. Pour the mixture over the popcorn and mix thoroughly. Place popcorn mixture onto a baking pan and bake at 250 degrees for 50 minutes. To cool, remove from the pan and place on waxed paper.

Port Angeles Snack Attack
2 7-inch flour tortillas
2 Tablespoons strawberry cream cheese
¼ cup of raisins
¼ cup of dried cranberries
1 cup finely chopped green apples
1 teaspoon sugar and cinnamon combined

Directions: Finely chop apples and place them in a medium sized bowl. Add cranberries, raisins, and sugar cinnamon mixture and stir. Then, fry the tortilla with one tablespoon of margarine in a skillet till crisp. Place tortilla on a paper towel to take off excess margarine and to cool. Once cooled, spread cream cheese and top with apple concoction.

Sugar Cookies
1 cup butter
¼ cup of milk
1 teaspoon vanilla
4 cups flour

2 eggs
1 ½ cups granulated sugar
1 teaspoon baking soda

Directions: Cut butter into flour. Combine sugar, eggs, vanilla. Mix all ingredients together. Roll out onto a floured surface. Cut with an apple cookie cutter. Place on a baking sheet. Bake at 350 degrees for 8 to 10 minutes. Yields three dozen cookies.

Golden Oatmeal Cookies
1 cup, 2 sticks of unsalted butter, cooled to room temperature
¼ cup of vegetable shortening
1 cup light brown sugar
¾ cup of granulated sugar
2 large eggs
1 teaspoon vanilla extract
2 ½ cups rolled oats
2 cups all purpose flour
½ teaspoon baking soda
½ teaspoon salt
½ teaspoon ground cinnamon
1 cup dried dates, chopped

Directions: Preheat oven to 375 degrees. In a large bowl, beat the butter and shortening until smooth. Next, add the sugars, again, beating mixture until smooth. Add the eggs, one at a time as well as the vanilla, put aside. In a separate bowl, mix all of the dry ingredients, including the cinnamon. Once the dry ingredients have been mixed, combine the wet ingredients and mix until well combined. Then, stir in the dates. Drop the batter by rounded tablespoonfuls 1 ½ inches apart on a cookie sheet. Bake for 12 to 14 minutes.

Bella Chow Biscotti
¾ cup of butter
1-Cup of Sugar
2-eggs

1 ½ teaspoons vanilla extract
2 ½ cups flour
2 teaspoons of ground cinnamon
¾ teaspoon baking powder
½ teaspoon salt
Almond slices

Directions: In a large bowl, mix butter and sugar with an electric mixer, beating in the eggs one at a time. Next, add the vanilla extract and stir in the flour, baking powder, salt, cinnamon, and almonds. Cover the dough in the refrigerator and chill for ten minutes. Once chilled, take out of the refrigerator and divide the dough into two parts, roll into approximately 9 inch logs. Place the logs on a lightly greased cookie sheet; flatten the logs with our hands prior to baking the biscotti cookies. Bake in a 350 degree oven for 30 minutes. Take out of the oven, and cool for five minutes. While dough is still warm, with a sharp long knife, cut the dough in ½ to inch diagonal pieces. On the same cookie sheet, turn diagonal pieces on their sides and bake for an additional 5 minutes in the same (350 degree oven). Makes about 3 dozen cookies.

First Love Chocolate Mousse
8 ounces of semi sweet chocolate chips
2 Tablespoons of strong coffee
2 Tablespoons of orange extract
1 Egg Yolk
2 Egg Whites
A pinch of salt
2 Tablespoons of Sugar
½ Cup Heavy Cream (or ½ carton of cool whip)

Directions: Melt the chocolate and coffee over low heat. When you remove from heat, add the orange extract and then the egg yolk, stirring till the mixture is smooth. In another bowl, beat the egg whites and salt, next add the sugar and beat with an electric mixture until stiff peaks form. Lastly, whip the cream until it is stiff and fold into the egg whites and then fold into the chocolate mixture. Place in the refrigerator, and chill until ready to serve.

Chocolate and Apricot Torte

½ cup of unsalted butter
1 cup of semi-sweet chocolate chips
5 large eggs, separated
¾ cup of sugar
1 cup ground Almonds
1/3 cup of dried apricots, finely chopped
Dried apricots and fresh strawberries for garnish

Directions: Melt chocolate chips and butter together in the top of a double boiler and cool. Beat the egg yolks with the sugar until they become pale yellow. Mix the cooled chocolate mixture into the eggs and sugar mixture, blending in the ground nuts. Add the chopped apricots too. Next, beat the egg whites until stiff, and fold into the chocolate mixture. Place a pan of water on the bottom shelf of a pre-heated 375 degree oven. Finally line the bottom and side of a 9 inch spring form pan with aluminum foil and place pan cooking spray on the aluminum foil. Pour in the batter and bake for 45 to 50 minutes. Remove from the oven and cool in the pan for 15 minutes. Release the sides of the pan and carefully place onto a serving plate. Peel off the foil and allow to cool completely. To serve, dust with ground almonds or powdered sugar. Garnish with strawberry halves and apricots.

*Placing a pan of water on the bottom shelf helps make the torte moist.

Love at First Sip (Beverages)

Love at First Sip Soda
1 box red Jell-O
2 liters red soda

Directions: Prepare the Jell-O according to the package directions. Chill overnight. Next, place the red punch into a punch bowl and add cut up pieces of Jell-O into the punch bowl.

Coke Slushy
Icee Maker
Rock Salt
Ice
2 Liters of Coke

Directions: Follow the directions provided with the icee maker. You could also try a snow cone maker machine, place ice in the snow cone maker, move the button to finely chopped ice, then add coke cola.

"As always, I was electrically aware of Edward sitting close enough to touch, as distant as if he were merely an invention of my imagination."- Bella

Invention of My Imagination
Orange Juice
1 Banana
7-up or Sprite
Strawberry soda
Optional: ice

Directions: Combine orange juice, sliced banana, 7-Up and strawberry soda in a punch bowl. You may also do a variation of this concoction by placing all ingredients in a blender and adding some ice.

Bella lost her appetite so she only got a bottle of lemonade to drink for lunch.

Lemonade Slushy
Lemonade
7-UP or Sprite soda
Lime to garnish
Optional: ice

Directions: Mix all ingredients in a punch bowl, serve.

"Good luck tended to avoid me."-Bella

Blushing Bella
Strawberry Mango juice
Lemonade
Lime to garnish

Directions: Mix all ingredients in a punch bowl, serve.

Bella Temple
Red raspberry
Mango juice
7-Up or Sprite

Directions: Mix all ingredients in a punch bowl, serve.

Werewolf Brew
3 cups apricot nectar
3 cups pineapple or orange juice
4 cups ginger ale or 7-up
2 cups orange or lemon sherbet

Directions: In a large bowl, combine the apricot and pineapple juices. Just before serving, add the chilled ginger ale. Pour into glasses and top with tiny scoops of sherbet.

Pomegranate Tea Recipe
¾ cup of instant tea
2/3 cup of pomegranate juice
½ cup instant orange drink such as Tang
1 teaspoon ground allspice
½ teaspoon cloves

Directions: Combine ingredients and mix thoroughly. Stir in one Tablespoon of mix per cup of water. Makes 1 ¾ cups of mix.

Vampire Venom Punch
1 can (6 ounces) frozen lemonade concentrate, thawed
1 can (6 ounces) frozen limeade concentrate, thawed
1 can (20 ounces) pineapple chunks, not drained
2 cups of water
2 liters of cherry soda, chilled
2 liters of ginger ale, chilled
Sliced lemon and lime slices

Directions: In a blender, mix concentrates as well as pineapple, until smooth. Next, stir in water. In a punch bowl, add sodas and frozen pineapple mixture. Garnish with lemon and lime slices.

Vampire Blood Punch
One 10 ounce package of frozen raspberries in syrup, thawed
4 cups of pineapple juice
One six ounce can of frozen lemonade concentrate, thawed
One bottle of 7-Up
Ice cubes
Lemon or lime slices for garnish

Directions: In a punch bowl add thawed raspberries, lemonade concentrate and the other remaining ingredients. Garnish with lemon or lime slices, or both.

Pomme Punch, that's French for apple
1 14oz. can of sweetened condensed milk
1 46oz. can pineapple juice, chilled

1 2-liter bottle of strawberry soda, chilled
Raspberry sherbet ice cream.

Directions: In a punch bowl, clean caldron container, stir together sweetened condensed milk, pineapple juice, and strawberry soda. Top with sherbet and serve over ice.

"His fingers were ice-cold, like he'd been holding them in a snowdrift before class."-Bella

Ice-cold Finger Punch
2 cans of red concentrated red punch
1 liter of 7-up or Lemon Lime Soda
2 latex gloves

Directions: Fill two latex gloves with water and tie off the ends with a rubber band and place into the freezer. In a punch bowl, mix 7-up with 2 cans of red punch, add water according to the punch directions. When the latex gloves are frozen, take the "hand" out of the glove and add to the punch bowl. You will have floating hands, and it will also serve to keep the punch cold.

Cup of Charlie
Coffee Maker
Paper filter for coffee maker (make sure it is the correct size for the specific coffee maker)
French Roast gourmet Coffee
Coffee grinder

Directions: In a coffee grinder place the desired amount of beans for brewing and grind. Next, place freshly ground coffee in paper filter in the coffee maker. Next, add water to coffee maker, the more water the weaker the coffee will be. The less water, the stronger the coffee will be. Turn on coffee maker and Walla, in a few minutes a cup of Charlie. May add sugar or creamer or store bought vanilla creamer to coffee.

Edward's Thirst Quencher
3 Large Ripe Peaches

3 Large Lemons
3 Large Oranges
1 Cup of Sugar
3 Cups of Strawberries
3 Cups of Raspberries
1 Two Liter Bottle of Ginger Ale, cold and chilled
Some ice cubes
15 to 20 Strawberries

Directions: Peel and section the lemons, and oranges and remove the peach skins and pits, and cut them into thin slices. Next, place the peaches, lemons, oranges, and sugar into a blender. Pour into a punch bowl, add ginger ale and ice cubes. Float strawberries and orange slices on top of Edward's Thirst Quencher.

Wolf bane On the rocks Orange Julius
1/2 cup of orange juice, without pulp
1/2 cup of sunny delight
1 Tablespoon of Vanilla Extract
¾ cup of ice
1 Tablespoon of Granulated Sugar

Directions: In a blender place all of the ingredients. Blend on medium speed until ice has been crushed and Julius is frothy. May add more ice and or orange juice as needed.

Virgin Bloody Mary
One 46 ounce bottle of chilled tomato juice
3 tablespoons horseradish
3 tablespoons of freshly squeezed lemon juice
1 teaspoon of Tabasco sauce
¾ of a teaspoon of Worcestershire sauce
Ice cubes

Directions: In a large pitcher, combine tomato juice, lemon juice, and Tabasco, horseradish, and Worcestershire sauce. Stir until well blended.

Next, fill 8-10 glasses with mixture, adding ice, a lemon wedge or celery stalk. May sprinkle with pepper.

Twilight Tribute Punch
2 10 ounce packages of frozen strawberries, defrosted
1 6 ounce can of lemonade concentrate, thawed
1 quart of ginger ale
2 cups of raisins
6 gummy worms

Directions: Mix strawberries and lemonade concentrate in a blender until smooth. Add ginger ale and then transfer the beverage into a punch bowl. Stir in raisins and ginger ale. Place gummy worms on the side of the bowl.

Eclipse
1 cup black cherry
1 cup of cranberry juice
1 cup ginger ale
splash of pineapple juice

Directions: Mix black cherry, cranberry juice, and ginger ale in a punch bowl, Add a splash of pineapple juice, and serve over ice.

New Moon Punch
1 gallon cranberry juice
1 gallon orange juice
1 cup raspberry sorbet
1 quart seltzer
Plastic vampire teeth

Directions: Mix the juices together. Add the sorbet, softened, and stir until it disappears. Add the seltzer. May float plastic vampire teeth in punch bowl.

Howl at Twilight Cocktails

Increments

1 cup	8 ounces
1 split	6.3 ounces
1 wineglass	4 ounces
1 pony	1 ounce
1 dash	1/32 ounce
1 jigger	1 ½ ounces

"Don't you want to know if I drink blood?"-Edward talking to Bella

Breathless
1/2 lime
1/2 ounce white crème de cacao
1/2 ounce cointreau
1 ounce white Jamaica rum
Club Soda

Directions: Squeeze lime juice into a glass filled with ice cubes; save lime shell. Add to glass crème de cacao, cointreau, and rum. Add Club soda to fill glass. Stir. Decorate with lime shell and fresh mint dusted with bar sugar.

Scotch & Water

Directions: Pour 1 to 1 1/2 ounces scotch over ice cubes in a 14-ounce Highball glass. Serve a small pitcher of water alongside.

Bloody Mary
One 46 ounce bottle of chilled tomato juice
3 tablespoons horseradish
3 tablespoons of freshly squeezed lemon juice
1 teaspoon of Tabasco sauce
¾ of a teaspoon of Worcestershire sauce
1 ½ cups of vodka

Ice cubes

Directions: In a large pitcher, combine tomato juice, lemon juice, Tabasco, horseradish, Worcestershire, and vodka. Stir until well blended. Next, fill 8-10 glasses with mixture, adding ice, a lemon wedge or celery stalk. May sprinkle with pepper.

Never Die
½ ounce of rum
½ ounce of dry vermouth
½ ounce of gin
½ ounce of sloe gin
½ ounce of triple sec
½ ounce of vodka
½ ounce of whiskey
6 ounces of coke a cola or Hawaiian Punch

Directions: In shaker with ice, add the ingredients, strain. Add a cherry with a pineapple or Orange slice as garnish.

Gin and Tonic
Tonic Water
A shot of Gin
A twist of lemon or lime

Wicked Gin and Tonic
Fill glass with ice
1 shot Gin or Vodka

Directions: Remainder of glass, fill with Tonic water

Bad Vampire
1 part vodka
1 part Tia Maria

Directions: Stir with ice cubes. Strain into chilled cocktail glass.

Twilight Run Cocktail
1/2 ounce French vermouth
1/2 ounce Italian vermouth
1 ounce brandy
1/4 ounce Pernod
1/2 teaspoon Curacao

Directions: Stir well with ice cubes. Strain into 3-ounce cocktail glass.

Midnight Stroll Punch
1 quart brandy
1 quart sweet sherry
4 ounces maraschino liqueur
1/2 pint Curacao
4 quarts champagne
2 quarts club soda
Sliced fresh fruits
Halved seeded grapes

Directions: Pre chill all liquid ingredients. Pour into a punch bowl add cubed ice and fruits. Serve punch in champagne glasses. Serves 35 to 40 people.

Forkshattan
1 ½ ounces of blended whiskey
½ ounce of sweet vermouth

Directions: Place whiskey and sweet vermouth in a shaker with ice and strain. For a dry Manhattan, use dry vermouth and garnish with an olive.

Jasper Cocktail
1 ounce sweet sherry
1/2 ounce Italian vermouth
1 dash orange bitters

Directions: Shake with ice cubes. Strain into chilled cocktail glass.

Alice Cullen Cocktail
2 ounces Pernod
1/2 lump sugar

Directions: Half fill cocktail glass with shaved ice. Place sugar on top. Drip Pernod on sugar. Add a twist of lemon peel, and serve with cut straws.

Cafe de Amore
1 1/2 ounces of gin
1 egg white
1 teaspoon Pernod or Herbsaint
1 teaspoon of fresh cream

Directions: Shake well with ice cubes. Strain into chilled 4-ounce cocktail glasses.

Enchanted
1 ounce cognac
1/4 ounce green Chartreuse
1 teaspoon lemon juice
2 drops Angostura bitters

Directions: Shake with ice cubes. Strain into a chilled cocktail glass.

Cullen Cocktail
1 ounce of Red Rum
Coke or Pepsi
Lime as garnish

Directions: Fill a glass with ice cubes and coke or Pepsi soda. Squeeze lime into the glass, Add the rum, and stir.

Rum and Coke
1 ounce of Rum
Coke or Pepsi

Directions: Add ice cubes to a glass. Next, add coke or Pepsi and rum. Stir. If sugar Content is of concern, you may use diet Coke or diet Pepsi. For an added zing, use flavored colas such as Vanilla or Cherry Coke.

Isabella Crown and Coke
1 ounce of Crown Rum
Coca Cola

Directions: Add ice cubes to a glass. Next, add the coke and Crown Rum. Stir and serve.

Bella Italiano Cocktail
1 ounce absinthe
1/2 ounce anisette
3 dashed maraschino liqueur
1/4 ounce water

Directions: Shake with ice cubes. Strain into chilled cocktail glass.

Just A Dream
3/4 ounce evaporated milk
3/4 ounce white crème de cacao
3/4 ounce Crème de Noyaux

Directions: Mix ingredients and Shake with ice cubes. Strain into a cocktail glass.

Shimmer
1 ounce Barbados rum
1 ounce Grand Marnier
1/2 ounce fresh cream

Directions: Shake with ice cubes. Strain into chilled cocktail glass.

White Cloud
3/4 ounce vodka
1/2 ounce white crème de cacao
1 dash evaporated milk
1 dash Lopez coconut cream

Directions: Shake with ice cubes. Strain into chilled cocktail glass.

Around the World
3 ounces orange juice
3 ounces lemon juice
3 ounces light Puerto Rican rum
1/2 ounce brandy
Juice of 1/2 fresh lime

Directions: Blend with 2 scoops of shaved ice for 12 to 15 seconds in an electric mixer. Pour into two large glasses. Fill glasses with cracked ice. Serve with straws. Makes 2 drinks.

Grandma Marie
1 1/2 ounces light Puerto Rican rum
2 ounces orange juice
Angostura bitters

Directions: Pour rum and orange juice over ice cubes in an old fashioned style glass.
Stir. Float a few drops of bitters on top.

Bella Brandy
1 ounce of Brandy
1 ounce of Crème de Cacao
1 ounce of heavy cream
½ cup of ice

Directions: Combine all ingredients in a blender. Blend for about a minute. Top with cocoa powder, cinnamon, or nutmeg, or a combination of the three.

Forks Cooler
Juice of 1/2 lemon
1/4 teaspoon sugar
2 ounces of New England rum
Club soda

Directions: Shake lemon juice, sugar, and rum with ice cubes. Strain into a goblet. Add ice cubes. Fill with soda. Add a dash of rum on top.

Phil's Highball
2 ounces Bourbon
Ginger ale

Directions: Pour Bourbon over ice cubes in a highball glass. Fill with ginger ale. Add a twist of lemon peel. Stir.

Fast Pitch
2 ounces brandy
Ginger ale or club soda

Directions: Pour brandy over 1 ice cube in an 8-ounce highball glass. Fill with ginger ale or club soda. Add a twist of lemon peel. Stir gently.

Charlie Swan Sergeant Drink
4 ounces brandy
2 dashes Pernod
3 dashes Angostura bitters
1 teaspoon lemon juice
1 teaspoon sugar syrup
1 egg
Club soda

Directions: Shake all ingredients except soda with ice cubes. Strain into tall Highball glasses. Add ice cubes. fill glass with soda. Dust with grated nutmeg.

Morning Glory Margaritas
(Makes 8-10 margaritas)
1 lime, cut into 8-10 wedges
8-10 toothpicks
8-10 maraschino cherries
1 pint of Tequila
1 cup of orange liqueur, such as Triple Sec
1 cup freshly squeezed lime juice
Ice cubes
Rock (coarse salt), to rim the margarita glasses

Directions: In a pie tin, place salt. Rub the rims of the margarita glasses with lime juice (may use lemon juice). Dip the rims of each glass into the salt. Next, combine the tequila, orange liqueur, lime juice and ice into a blender. Blend the mixture. On a toothpick, place cherry and small lime wedge. Pour into the margarita glasses and garnish with lime and a cherry. For a sweeter margarita, add flavoring, such as strawberry and rim the glass with sugar.

Love At First Sight Cocktail
1 1/2 ounces gin
4 dashes grenadine
Juice of 1/2 lime or lemon
1 egg white

Directions: Shake with ice cubes. Strain into a chilled double cocktail glass. Decorate with a mint leaf.

Moonlight
Juice of 1 lemon
1/2 tablespoon bar sugar
2 ounces calvados or applejack
Club soda

Directions: Shake lemon juice, sugar, and calvados with ice cubes. Strain into highball glass. Add 1 ice cube. Fill glass with soda. Decorate with sliced fresh fruit.

1/2 teaspoon grenadine
Club soda or ginger ale
2 ounces French vermouth
Spiral-cut lemon or orange peel

Directions: Stir grenadine and 2 ounces soda or ginger ale together in a 12-ounce glass. Fill glass with ice cubes. Add vermouth. Fill with soda or ginger ale, and stir again. Insert lemon or orange spiral, and dangle
end over rim of glass.

Cullen Club Collins
1 ounce of Chambord
2 ounces of Sweet and sour

Directions: Fill the glass with club soda and add ice. May garnish with lime and a cherry.

Breaking Dawn Glory
2 ounces scotch or Bourbon
2 dashes Pernod
1 egg white
1 teaspoon bar sugar
Juice of 1/2 lemon
Juice of 1/2 lime
Club soda

Directions: Shake all ingredients except soda with ice cubes. Strain into chilled large goblet. Fill glass with soda.

Holiday Eggnog
12 eggs, separated
2 cups bar sugar
1 teaspoon vanilla
1 1/2 gallons cold milk

1 pint brandy
1 cup Jamaica rum
Grated nutmeg

Directions: Beat egg yolks until thick; gradually add 1 1/2 cups of the sugar, and mix until thick and lemon colored. Next, blend in vanilla and milk. Stir in brandy and rum, pouring them into milk mixture very slowly. With clean beaters, beat egg whites until soft peaks form; gradually add remaining sugar, and beat until egg whites are stiff. Spoon egg whites over the top of the milk mixture, and sprinkle with nutmeg. Serves 30 to 35 people.

"Your mood swings are kinda giving me whiplash." -Bella

Milky Way
1/2 ounce brandy
1/2 ounce Jamaica rum
1/2 ounce Bourbon
6 ounces milk
3 drops vanilla
    Directions: Shake well in commercial electric drink mixer with a large scoop of Ice cubes. Pour into a 10-ounce glass. Add ice cubes to almost
Fill glass. Dust with grated nutmeg. Serve with a straw.

Arizona Comfort
Juice of 1/2 lemon
1/2 teaspoon bar sugar
2 ounces Southern Comfort
Club soda

Directions: Shake lemon juice, sugar, and Southern Comfort with ice cubes. Strain into a highball glass. Add 2 ice cubes. Fill glass with soda.

Baseball Cocktail
1 ounce gin
1/2 ounce French vermouth
2 dashes Angostura bitters

Directions: Stir with ice cubes. Strain into chilled cocktail glass. Add an olive.

Love At First Sip
1/2 ounce Benedictine
1 1/2 ounce Bourbon

Directions: Stir with ice cubes. Strain into chilled cocktail glass. Add a twist of lemon peel.

Breaking Dawn
1/2 ounce lemon juice
1/2 ounce cointreau
1/2 ounce white crème de cacao
1/2 ounce gin
1/2 ounce scotch or Bourbon

Directions: Shake with ice cubes. Strain into chilled tiki stem champagne glass or other large saucer champagne glass.

Mai Tai
1 lime
1/2 ounce orange Curacao
1/4 ounce rock candy syrup
1 ounce dark Jamaica rum
1 ounce Martinique rum

Directions: Cut lime in half; squeeze juice over shaved ice in a mai tai glass; save one shell. Add remaining ingredients and enough shaved ice to fill glass. Hand shake. Decorate with spent lime shell, and fresh mint.

Million Dollar Cocktail
2 teaspoons pineapple juice
1 teaspoon grenadine
1 egg white
3/4 ounce Italian vermouth
1 1/2 ounces gin

Directions: Shake well with ice cubes. Strain into chilled large cocktail glass.

Dry Martini
1 ounce gin
1/4 ounce French vermouth
1/2 teaspoon Pernod

Directions: Stir with ice cubes. Strain into chilled cocktail glass. Decorate with a pearl cocktail onion.

Little Red Chevy Truck
1 1/2 ounces Vodka
Juice of 1/4 lime
7-Up

Directions: Pour vodka and lime juice over ice cubes in an old fashioned glass or glass mug. Fill glass with 7-Up.

Lemon Drop
1 ½ ounces of plain or lemon vodka
¾ ounce of fresh lemon juice
1 teaspoon of sugar

Directions: Place lemon vodka and freshly squeezed lemon juice into a shaker with plenty of ice. Add sugar and shake. Stain into a chilled cocktail glass. Can also line the rim of the glass with lemon juice (to make it stick) and sugar.

"How you likin' the rain, girl?" -Mike Newton

Bone Shaker
2 ounces of VooDoo Spiced Rum
½ ounce of triple sec
½ ounce of lime juice
3 ounces of pineapple juice

Directions: Blend with crushed ice, and garnish with a lime wedge and a cherry.

Pucker Up Collins
½ ounce of Sour Apple Puckers
½ ounce of Peach Puckers
½ ounce of Tropical Fruit Puckers
2 ounces of sweet and sour.

Directions: Fill a glass with club soda. Next, add a cherry.

Twilight Time for a Party Punch

6 ounces concentrated orange juice, thawed
2 cans pineapple juice
1 cup lemon juice
1 cup sugar
2 bottles of champagne
1 bottle of Chablis

Directions: Mix and keep cold. Just before serving, add 2 bottles of champagne and 1 bottle of chilled Chablis.

"You are my life now."-Edward

Bella Loves Edward Punch
¼ cup of Vodka
½ gallon of raspberry sherbet
2 bottles of pink champagne
2 cans of 7-Up

Directions: Mix and keep cold. Just before serving, add 2 bottles of pink champagne, vodka and sherbet.

Vampire Kiss Cherry Punch
1 can (6 ounces) frozen lemonade concentrate, thawed
1 can (6 ounces) frozen limeade concentrate, thawed
1 can (20 ounces) pineapple chunks, undrained
2 cups of water
2 liters of cherry soda, chilled
2 liters of ginger ale, chilled
Sliced lemon and lime slices

Directions: In a blender, mix concentrates as well as pineapple, until smooth. Next, stir in water. In a punch bowl, add sodas and frozen pineapple mixture. Garnish with lemon and lime slices.

Raspberry Pineapple Crush Punch
One 10 ounce package of frozen raspberries in syrup, thawed
4 cups of pineapple juice
One six ounce can of frozen lemonade concentrate, thawed
One bottle of 7-Up
Ice cubes

Directions: In a blender, mix concentrate as well frozen raspberries, until smooth. Next, stir in water. In a punch bowl, add sodas and frozen pineapple juice. Garnish with lemon and lime slices.

Cutting Down On the Fat Content

Instead of:	Try:
Frying	Boiling, steaming, poaching, or stir frying
White Rice	Brown Rice
Sour Cream	Non-fat plain yogurt
Nuts, which tend to be fatty	Water chestnuts

Ways to Lighten Up a Recipe

If you are on a restricted diet, or are looking for ways to reduce fat in your daily eating regime, here are some suggestions.

If a recipes calls for:	Substitute:
Butter	Margarine, or butter flavored shortening
All-purpose flour	Unbleached flour or wheat flour
Dark brown sugar	Light brown sugar
Whole eggs	Brown eggs or liquid egg substitute
Oil	Applesauce
Chocolate	Carob
Olive oil	Vegetable or cooking spray oil
Lard	Shortening or butter

No time for a Supermarket Run

Substitutions

If you are out of…	**Substitute:**
1 Tablespoon of baking powder	1 teaspoon of baking soda and 2 teaspoons of cream of tartar
1 Tablespoon of cornstarch	2 Tablespoons of flour
1 cup of milk	½ cup of evaporated milk mixed with ½ cup of water.
1 cup buttermilk	1 cup of regular milk plus 1 Tablespoon of vinegar or lemon juice
1 cup of sugar	1 cup of honey, then reduce other Liquid ingredients in recipe by ¼ of a cup.

Weights and Measures

Equals	**Same as**
1 pound of sugar	Equals 2 cups of Sugar
1 pound of brown sugar	2 ½ cups of packed brown sugar
1 cup of granulated sugar	1 1/3 cups of granulated sugar

1 pound of powdered sugar	3 ½ cups of powdered sugar
1 pound of all purpose flour	4 cups of flour
12 egg yolks	1 cup of egg yolks
8-10 egg whites	1 cup of egg whites
A dash equals	slightly less than 1/8 of a teaspoon
3 teaspoons	1 Tablespoon
2 Tablespoons	1/8 cup, or 1 ounce
4 Tablespoons	¼ cup, 2 ounces
5 1/3 Tablespoons	1/3 cup
8 Tablespoons	½ cup
10 2/3 Tablespoons	2/3 cup
12 Tablespoons	¾ cup
14 Tablespoons	7/8 of a cup
16 Tablespoons	1 cup or ½ pint, 8 ounces
2 cups	1 pint
2 pints	1 quart
2 cups	16 ounces

OUNCES

½ fluid ounce	15 milliliters

2 fluid ounces	60 milliliters
8 fluid ounces	240 milliliters
16 fluid ounces	480 milliliters
1/8 cup	30 grams
¼ cup	60 grams
1 cup	240 grams
1 pound	480 grams

Cooking Terms and Translations

Braise
 To braise is to brown whatever one is preparing and to cook and cover it in its' own fat, using the liquids to preserve the juices.

Caramelize
To caramelize means to melt sugar slowly until it becomes brown and sticky.

Blaze
To blaze is to pour warmed liqueur or brandy over food, such as cherries jubilee and then light on fire.

Julienne
To julienne something, such as carrots or celery, is to cut into match like sticks.

Marinate
To marinate is to let stand in a seasoned liquid for flavor or tenderness. The marinade can be placed in a large plastic bag or poured over the food item to be marinated.

To knead is to work a mixture with your hands.

To scald is to heat milk until tiny bubbles appear.

Index

Apple Bread, 43
Apple Cider Cheese Fondue, 41
Apple Cider Spice, 42
Apple of My Eye Pie, 41
Arizona Corn Bake, 20
Artichoke Cheese Squares, 12
Bagel Bites, 12
Bat Chips, 9
Beef Stew, 21
Bella Chow Biscotti, 46
Bella's Instant Mashed Potatoes, 18
Bella Temple, 50
Bells' Lasagna, 29
Blushing Bella, 50
Blushing Bella Apples, 44
Broccoli Raisin Salad, 9
Broccoli Salad, 10
Butterscotch Bars, 37
Butterscotch Eyes, 38
Caesar Salad, 10
Cascade Mountain Mashed Potatoes, 18
Charlie's Catch of the day Crab Cakes, 14
Charlie's Dinner in a Skillet, 20
Charlie's fried eggs, 5
Cheese Enchiladas, 17
Chicken Cacciatore, 27
Chicken Enchiladas, 16
Chief Swan Salad, 11
Chocolate and Apricot Torte, 48
Chunky Applesauce, 42
Club Sandwich, 6
Cobb Salad, 11
Coke Slushy, 49
Corned Beef Sandwich, 6
Create your own Perfect Pizza, 27
Cup of Charlie, 52
Dare to Eat Dirt Pie, 37
Dare to Eat Mud Chocolate Pudding, 37
Easy Chicken Swan Parmesan, 30
Eclipse , 54
Edward's Thirst Quencher, 52
Eggs Bellentine, 6
Eggs Benedict, 5
Everyone Enjoys Different Flavors Sundae, 35
First Love Chocolate Mousse, 47

Forbidden Love Coconut Lemon Crumb Squares, 33
Fried Apples, 43
Get out the Forks Lemon Pie, 40
Golden Oatmeal Cookies, 46
Ham and Apple Sandwich, 7
Harry's Famous Fish Fry, 15
Hot Mulled Apple Cider, 42
Ice-cold Finger Punch, 52
I Dare You American Apple Crisp, 43
I Dare You to Eat Pizza Edward
Invention of My Imagination, 49
Irritated Grizzly Bear Steaks, 19
Jacob Blacks Grilled Cheese Sandwich, 7
Jasper Cookie Bars, 33
Lemonade Slushy, 50
Lion and the Lamb Stew, 14
Lobster Salad, 12
Love at First Bite Cupcakes, 38
Love at First Sip Soda, 49
Melt in your Mouth Coq au Vin , 23
Midnight Frosting, 41
Monster Eggs, 8
Mushroom Ravioli , 24
New Moon Punch, 54
Pasta with Broccoli and Artichokes, 28
Pasta with Creamy Garlic and Walnut Sauce, 26
Perfect for the Prom Bella's Bonbons, 34
Pomegranate Tea Recipe, 51
Pomme Punch, that's French for apple, 51
Port Angeles Snack Attack, 45
Pot Roast with vegetables, 19
Red Velvet Cake, 32
Rocky Road Brownies, 40
Salad a la Cullen, 9
Sink Your Teeth into Peanut Butter Pie, 34
South of the Phoenix Border Casserole, 22
Spaghettini Primavera, 28
Starry Night Cake , 35
Steak and Potatoes, 18
Stir Fry ala Swan, 13
Sugar Cookies, 45
Taco Soup, 21
Tallerina, 24
Time for Tea Cake Cookies, 31
Too Hot to Handle, 45
Tuna Sandwich, 8

Twilight Chocolate Cake, 36
Twilight Tribute Punch, 54
Vampire Bite Bars, 39
Vampire Bites, 39
Vampire Blood Punch, 51
Vampire Cupcakes, 44
Vampire Venom Punch, 51
Veal Scaloppini, 26
Virgin Bloody Mary, 53
Werewolf Brew, 50
Werewolf Chow, 44
Why the Traffic Jam Cookies, 31
Wolf bane On the rocks Orange Julius, 53
You'll need to Get Out the Forks Baked Beans, 22
Zucchini Relleno, 25

Cocktails Index

Alice Cullen Cocktail, 58
Arizona Comfort, 64
Around the World, 60
Bad Vampire, 56
Baseball Cocktail, 64
Bella Brandy, 60
Bella Italiano Cocktail, 59
Bella Loves Edward Punch, 68
Bloody Mary, 55
Bone Shaker, 67
Breaking Dawn, 65
Breaking Dawn Glory, 63
Breathless, 55
Cafe de Amore, 58
Charlie Swan Sergeant Drink, 61
Cullen Club Collins, 63
Cullen Cocktail, 58
Dry Martini, 66
Enchanted, 58
Fast Pitch, 61
Forks Cooler, 61
Forkshattan, 57
Gin and Tonic, 56
Grandma Marie, 60
Holiday Eggnog, 63
Jasper Cocktail, 57
Just A Dream, 59
Isabella Crown and Coke, 59

Lemon Drop, 66
Little Red Chevy Truck, 66
Love At First Sight Cocktail, 62
Love At First Sip, 65
Mai Tai, 65
Midnight Stroll Punch, 57
Milky Way, 64
Million Dollar Cocktail, 65
Moonlight, 62
Morning Glory Margaritas, 62
Never Die, 56
Phil's Highball 61
Pucker Up Collins, 67
Raspberry Pineapple Crush Punch, 68
Rum and Coke, 58
Scotch & Water, 55
Shimmer, 59
Twilight Run Cocktail, 57
Twilight Time for a Party Punch, 67
Vampire Kiss Cherry Punch, 68
White Cloud, 60
Wicked Gin and Tonic

Twilight Party Planning Guide

Pick a Scene from the Twilight movie. Chose your favorite moment: the baseball scene, perhaps the Prom scene, maybe Bella meeting the Cullens for the first time. Perhaps, host Your Own Twilight Movie Awards Night, dress up in fine evening wear and have your friends make their picks with your preprinted ballot. Decorate doorways, the birthday room, the front door, the kitchen, even outside if your party will be outdoors. Decorate with streamers, Twilight posters and colorful balloons. You could personalize your event by baking your own cake from a recipe found in *Bite At Twilight* or order a specialty theme cake or seek ideas from websites on how to create your own original memorable cake.

Twilight Party Checklist

Cards

Invitations (e-cards or regular card invitations)

Gift wrap (solid black, or red wrapping paper)

Thank you notes

Colored Ribbon to go with the theme

Tape

Name tags

Decorations

Streamers

Cups, utensils (just forks, might be a cute idea), and plates

Hats (baseball caps if you are choosing the baseball scene for your party)

Balloons and a Helium Tank

Mylar Balloons (Apple mylars)

Centerpieces (such as a bowl of apples)

Noisemakers

Confetti

Napkins

Party Favors

Banners and Wall decorations

Activities

Twilight DVD

Twilight Music and Clare De Lune

Games

Piñata

Craft paper

Crayons, paints, markers

Food

Drinks

Snacks

Cake and goodies

Main Course

Camera and batteries

Countdown to your Twilight Party

4 Weeks before the party

Select the day, time, and location

Chose the specific scene for your Twilight Theme

Make a guest list (gather email addresses)

Schedule a bounce house (if desiring one)

2-3 weeks

Send out invitations

Plan for the activities, decorations, and food

1 week prior to your Twilight Party

Shop for decorations, favors, supplies, and presents

Purchase a helium tank, order cake

If making a piñata, start now

3-5 days before party

Email friends to get a head count

Confirm location, pay any deposits, fill piñata with candy/packaged fruit snacks or mini presents

2 Days before party

Decorate party areas

Day of party

Prepare punch and food

Pick up cake/or finish decorating cake

Pick up Mylar balloons or fill your own balloons

Bella's Prom Primer Checklist

Things to Consider:

Plan your prom budget

Search online and through fashion magazines for form flattering styles, latest news, and newest styles.

Decide who you are going with. Do you feel comfortable asking the love of your life Edward, or will you be taking a friend such as Jacob?

Start making arrangements for hair, nail, and makeup appointments.

Take your girlfriends out to the mall to pick matching accessories such as shoes, jewelry, purse, and if it is anticipated that it will be cold, perhaps a shawl (or maybe Edward will let you wear his coat?)

If you will be renting a vehicle, decide what kind, how large, if it is a limousine, see if friends will be pitching in. You know how fast Edwards drives and how cute his car is, so maybe not a limo this time.

Purchase the prom dress.

Order Edward or Jacob's boutonnière.

Remind Edward or Jacob what color you'll be wearing so he chooses the right color and style of corsage.

Four Months Before the Prom

It is never too early to start looking for a dress.

Three Months Before the Prom

Brainstorm who is available and who you'd like to take as your date, or who you'd like to ask you.

Create a Budget, the prom is expensive, maybe start asking your boss for a few extra hours, or do a few extra chores around the house to see if your parents will chip in.

Sign up for an Etiquette class or brush up on your manners by reading a book or checking if your local church is putting on a fashion show or manners class.

Look in magazines and clip out pictures of different hairstyles. There are even online programs whereby you can upload your photo and try on different hairstyles without going to the hairdresser and making it permanent.

Two Months Before the Prom

Go on an out of town trip to the garment district and try factory outlet dresses. San Francisco, for instance, has a gunne sax outlet with merchandise reduced by as much as 75% off retail. If you can't find anything that you love, consider patronizing the local bridal boutique in your area. If all else fails, order a dress online, get your measurements taken at a bridal, prom outlet, or local fabric store.

Check out the tux shop with your date. If you want his cumber bun to match your dress, you might want to bring a swatch of the dress to the tux shop.

Make your hair and manicure and pedicure appointments. If you are getting your makeup done professionally, start checking out the different makeup companies that offer makeup and find out if they charge a flat rate or if you need to purchase the products.
Work on obtaining your accessories such as shoes, jewelry, purse.

Discuss your pre and post prom plans. If your plans involve a limousine, or a fancy restaurant, make sure your date has reserved both.

30 Days Before the Prom

Have your dress professionally altered, if it needs alterations.
Start walking around the house in your shoes, so they aren't a shock on your feet the day of the prom. Purchase blister ointment if needed.
Order the boutonniere from your local floral shop. If your date is ordering your corsage from the same shop, maybe you can get a discount for ordering the two from the same place. At the very least, you can make sure they match accordingly.

Two Weeks Before the Prom

Purchase the prom bids.

Bella's Prom Day Dos!

Pick up your date's boutonniere

Prepare your purse with the essentials

Make sure you or your date has possession of the prom bids

If your school requires identification, make sure you and your date have proper identification.

If your school has certain rules such as dress and hair codes make sure your date is in compliance with those restrictions.

Have a wonderful time!

Prom Purse Essentials

Breath spray, tic tacs or mints

Money

Cell phone

Cell phone charger

Mini sewing kit

Bobby pins, mini hairspray-

Prescription glasses or contacts, if needed

Safety pins

Powder

Shimmer blush

Mini perfume or perfume sample

Emergency mini deodorant

Extra panty hose

For inclusion in future editions or to learn how to publish your own manuscript: serendipitypressinc@gmail.com or write to PO Box 26734 Fresno, Ca. 93729, please include a self addressed stamped envelope.

About the Author

Gina Meyers graduated with a Bachelor of Science degree in Business/Marketing from California State University, Fresno and also has her emergency teaching credential. She lives in the Central Valley with her graphic designer husband David and son and daughter. This is Gina's fifth book. Her first three titles are about the ever enchanting, magical sitcom, *Bewitched*, which have sold over 3,000 copies worldwide. Gina has worked for two fortune 500 companies: Xerox and Google, and has been a consultant for Columbia Pictures Television, Nickelodeon, and her books and cooking expertise were featured in the television show Fanatical. Gina owns Serendipity Media, a promotions, publishing, and marketing firm. She also writes a cooking column for Examiner.com. Her website is: www.unofficialtwilightcookbook.blogspot.com. She is currently at work on her next book.

www.ingramcontent.com/pod-product-compliance
Lightning Source LLC
Chambersburg PA
CBHW081500040426

42446CB00016B/3324